Making Tabouli

traditional Lebanese food

Kerry Nagle

Australian Multicultural Foundation

Blake
EDUCATION
Better ways to learn

Acknowledgments

We would like to thank the Baini family for their contribution and participation.

Making Tabouli: traditional Lebanese food
ISBN: 1 74164 097 0

Written by Kerry Nagle
Copyright © 2006 Blake Publishing
Published by Blake Education Pty Ltd
ABN 50 074 266 023
108 Main Rd
Clayton South VIC 3168
Ph: (03) 9558 4433
Fax: (03) 9558 5433
email: mail@blake.com.au
Visit our website: www.blake.com.au

Harmony and Understanding program developed by UC Publishing Pty Ltd
Designer: Luke Sharrock
Series Editor: Hass Dellal
Editor: Kerry Nagle

Printed in Malaysia by Thumbprints Utd Sdn Bhd

Contents

In this book ...

Introduction

George's family comes from Lebanon.

George has two parents, two sisters and two brothers.

Like many families, they enjoy spending time together – cooking, eating and relaxing with games and music.

Country facts: Lebanon

- Lebanon is a small, Arabic country located on the eastern shore of the Mediterranean Sea.

- It is bordered by Syria in the north and east, with Israel in the south.

- Its capital is Beirut.

- Its population is about 3.5 million.

- Its official language is Arabic, but French and English are also spoken.

1 ALBANIA
2 BOSNIA and HERZEGOVINA
3 CROATIA
4 Former YUGOSLAV REPUBLIC of MACEDONIA
5 KOSOVO
6 SERBIA and MONTENEGRO
7 SLOVENIA

Migration

Over the years, Lebanese people have decided to leave their homeland for different reasons.

After World War II, many migrants left Lebanon for economic reasons, or because they wanted to live and work in a new country. After 1976, large numbers of Lebanese people migrated to other countries because of the civil war in their homeland.

George's grandparents migrated from Lebanon in the 1950s. They continue to teach their family about Lebanese culture and traditions.

Tabouli – a family favourite

Today, George and his family are going to make one of their favourite recipes – a salad called tabouli.

George's family has a special recipe for tabouli that has been passed down for many generations. When making the dish, they keep the tradition of involving the whole family.

Tabouli is considered one of the national dishes of Lebanon. It is a salad based on burghul wheat, tomato, mint and parsley. Other ingredients, such as olive oil and lemon juice, are used for flavouring.

Word fact
There are many other ways to spell tabouli: for example, tabouleh, taboule and taboli.

Preparing the ingredients

Every member of the family has a role. It is George's job to pick the parsley from the garden.

He needs to pick quite a lot, because it is one of the main ingredients of the salad. It is important to use fresh parsley for tabouli, so the salad will taste good.

Fast fact

Parsley is a hardy, biennial herb. It is native to the Mediterranean region. Parsley leaves were used by the ancient Greeks and Romans to flavour and decorate their food. Parsley leaves can be used either fresh or dried and are popular in many different dishes.

George gets all the ingredients together in the kitchen: tomatoes, parsley, lemons, spring onions, mint and burghul wheat.

George washes everything carefully. He shakes off the excess water from the parsley and removes the thick stalks. He wraps the parsley in a tea towel and places it in the refrigerator. This will make the parsley crisp and dry.

The burghul is placed in a bowl and covered with cold water for 30 minutes.

Then it is drained through a sieve, to get rid of as much moisture as possible, and placed in a mixing bowl.

Word fact
Burghul can be spelled in many different ways: for example, bulgur, burghoul, balgour and boulgur.

Burghul

- Making wheat into burghul is an ancient process that originated in the Mediterranean region more than 4000 years ago.

- In ancient times, burghul was made by boiling wheat in huge pots, sometimes for days, until it was cooked thoroughly.

- The wheat was then spread out to dry in the sun.

- Next, the hardened kernels of wheat were cracked into coarse pieces. They were then sieved into different sizes for various uses.

Chopping the ingredients

Rachel chops the tomatoes into squares and adds it to the burghul in the mixing bowl.

It is best to use very sharp knives on the ingredients, as tabouli is a very fine dish. The size of the pieces that go in the mix can greatly affect the outcome. On the other hand, it is important not to chop ingredients like parsley too finely, or it will become mushy.

Jasmine carefully cuts the parsley, mint and spring onions. This is also added to the burghul mixture.

Safety is important when cooking. George will have to wait until he is older before he is allowed to use sharp knives to cut up the ingredients.

Seasoning the salad

The last step is to season the salad.

Mark-Anthony helps squeeze the lemons. Then, George adds the juice to the mixture, being careful not to add too much.

18

George seasons the mixture with salt and pepper and Rachel adds a little bit of olive oil.

The mixture is stirred so that all the flavours blend together.

The Lebanese way

No matter where they live, Lebanese people enjoy spending time together with family and friends. Sharing good food is just one way to come together as a family.

Today, people around the world enjoy Lebanese food. Lebanese restaurants serve traditional and local foods so that people can experience a little of Lebanese culture.

Glossary

biennial   a plant that usually only lives two years and normally produces flowers and seed in the second year

burghul   wheat that has been cooked, dried and cracked

migrants   people who have moved from one country to another

pulses   seeds such as peas, beans and lentils that you can eat

pita bread   a round flat bread

tabouli   a Lebanese salad

seasoning   adding flavour

Index